THRIVING AS A

HAIR & BEAUTY

FREELANCER

"Ebru is truly an inspirational businesswoman. I could listen to her speak all day. Her passion for business and helping people really radiates every time she steps in front of a microphone."

– Sila Gatti, Founder, Not Coffee

"Ebru is an innovator and an inspiration to everyone who wants to turn impossible dreams into reality. I love it when she says my clients are not a transaction, it's an experience."

– Jason Cunningham, Co-Founder & Director, Head of Business Advisory

"When I heard Ebru speak at the International Women's Day event, I was inspired. Her genuine humility when she was sharing her story touched me and gave me someone to look up to. I loved her message, her kindness, and how her hard-earned success has given her the confidence to share her truth. What a woman!"

– Nat Binette, Therapeutic Listener & Well-Being Consultant

"Ebru's courage, wisdom, and go-getter attitude has been a beacon of inspiration for our business audience. She has that special entrepreneurial knack of innovation, which she wraps inside a philosophy of making life easier and better for those who use her products and services. And, she's one of those rare gems who has the ability to communicate her ideas—without the jargon—to a broad range of people."

– Chris Ashmore, Senior Producer, Sound Cartel

"Ebru Sak is inspirational! I am in awe of her resilience, capacity to love and encourage others to love themselves, her advocacy for women, her determination and commitment, her business acumen, her energy! Everyone should have a role model, friend, and cheerleader like Ebru in their life. And she's an awesome hairdresser!"

– Gaynor Richmond

"I feel blessed to have met Ebru. Her story shows courage, strength, and perseverance despite the sadness and pain she has endured. She is a person who has moved beyond and above, and soared to great heights to become the amazing, gracious, inspiring, spiritual, dynamic woman she is."

– Jan Rose

"Ebru is a truly inspirational woman and a valuable role model to other women. She has a special gift for uplifting people and making them feel beautiful."

– Chris Pratt

"Ebru is a woman of many talents, gifts and attributes, which she brings to every interaction with those who are fortunate enough to meet her."

– Brian James

"Ebru is an inspiration to everyone who has the pleasure of meeting her. I thank the Universe that we met. She was born to succeed and everything she touches turns to gold!"

– Natasha Kastropil, Strategic Account Manager

Published in Australia by
Saks Salons
PO Box 256, Doreen VIC 3754 Australia
Email: ebru@sakssalons.com.au
www.sakssalons.com.au

First published in Australia 2024
Copyright © Ebru Sak 2024

National Library of Australia Cataloguing in Publication entry

A catalogue record for this book is available from the National Library of Australia

ISBN: 978-0-9756275-0-1 (paperback)
ISBN: 978-0-9756275-1-8 (hardback)
ISBN: 978-0-9756275-2-5 (epub)

Cover photography by Koch Photography

Book layout and design by Sophie White Design

Printed by IngramSpark

All care has been taken in the preparation of the information herein, but no responsibility can be accepted by the publisher or author for any damages resulting from the misinterpretation of this work. All contact details given in this book were current at the time of publication, but are subject to change.

The advice given in this book is based on the experience of the individuals. Professionals should be consulted for individual problems. The author and publisher shall not be responsible for any person with regard to any loss or damage caused directly or indirectly by the information in this book.

Thriving as a
Hair & Beauty
Freelancer

The Ultimate Guide to Setting Up and
Running Your Own Business

EBRU SAK

To my beloved mother, Döne Sak, whose unwavering strength and endless love continue to inspire me. You taught me that even in the face of adversity, one's spirit remains unbreakable. This book is dedicated to your memory, a tribute to your legacy of empowering women and nurturing resilience. Forever in my heart.

ABOUT THE AUTHOR

"I believe you must bring your whole self to the table if you want to thrive in today's crazy world: your personality, your sense of humour and, most importantly, your heart."

– EBRU SAK

Ebru Sak stands at the forefront of the beauty industry as a distinguished Beauty Entrepreneur and Consultant, renowned for her founding ventures including Saks Salons and Marquage Cosmetics. With a wealth of over three decades in the hair and beauty domain, Ebru Sak has honed the art of navigating small business ventures to success. Her journey is a testament to resilience, having triumphed over formidable personal, cultural, and professional hurdles – from loss and rebuilding to emerging with even greater strength and prosperity.

Ebru authentically shares her inspirational experiences and stories with audiences in online and in-person events, interviews, and podcasts to shed light on what she is most passionate about – business, leadership, and empowering women.

For more information on Ebru, see **www.ebrusak.com**

CONTENTS

Dear Freelancer,

Welcome to a world where possibilities are boundless, and the freedom of being your own boss awaits you. I'm Ebru Sak, your mentor and the author of this comprehensive guide, *Thriving As A Hair And Beauty Freelancer*. It fills my heart with joy to embark on this journey with you – a journey that holds the promise of self-discovery, empowerment, and the path to becoming a flourishing hair and beauty freelancer.

My own story is woven with over three decades of hands-on experience in the hair and beauty industry – a tale that started as a salon owner and transformed into the rewarding realm of successful freelancing, coupled with a robust background in product research and development. One highlight I hold dear is my involvement in launching a groundbreaking cosmetic product that has left an indelible mark on the industry, DUO by EBRU.

Throughout my career, I've had the privilege of collaborating with extraordinary individuals and iconic brands. The knowledge and expertise amassed along the way are now at your disposal. From unravelling the complexities of the hair and beauty market to navigating the challenges and seizing the opportunities inherent in freelancing, my mission is to equip you with insights and guidance to excel in this dynamic field.

This guide goes beyond the basics, delving into advanced strategies, innovative approaches, and industry best-practices honed over the years. Success, in my belief, is rooted in a foundation of knowledge, continuous learning, and an unwavering passion for your craft. I encourage you to bring your curiosity, enthusiasm, and creativity to the forefront of your art.

Whether you are a dedicated stylist, makeup artist, or beauty therapist, this guide is crafted to provide you with the knowledge and tools to navigate the unique challenges and seize the abundant opportunities that come with being a self-employed solo flyer.

I penned these words for you – the eager freelancer ready to take control of your career and carve a lifestyle that aligns with your desires. It could be juggling family responsibilities, caring for a loved one, or embracing the freedom to travel and work at your own pace. Regardless of your unique circumstances, certain processes remain universal, requiring sound planning and execution. Let this guide be your companion when the road ahead seems uncertain, your inspiration on those challenging days.

My intention is to give back to an industry that has enriched my life. I want to share my experience and wisdom gained through start-up salons, freelancing, customer service, and product development, among other facets. Success, in my eyes, is about lifting others as you climb the ladder. This is my way of contributing to an industry for which I am deeply grateful. In this ever-changing field, embarking on my own path as an entrepreneur has not only granted me the freedom to shape my life but has also provided the means to raise my three daughters single-handedly, create a cosy home, drive the car of my dreams, and enjoy a sense of comfort and stability. It's been a journey filled with challenges and triumphs, but above all, it's brought me immense fulfillment and joy.

Now, I'm here to help fellow hair and beauty professionals overwhelmed with life's responsibilities see the possibility of living an exceptional life by bringing joy to customers through hair and beauty services.

The turning point for me came amidst tears in a pot of soup, a poignant moment when my dreams of a happily ever after were shattered. The abrupt end of my marriage left me in the depths of despair, but when you find yourself so far down with nowhere else to go, the only direction is up. I committed to getting back up, cutting through the tears, the dark and lonely nights, and the sole responsibility of raising my girls. It was undoubtedly a challenging journey marked by mistakes and poor choices, but here I am, ready to share my story and help you write your own tale of success.

So, sharpen your scissors, don your tool belt, and buckle-up for the transformative journey that awaits you as a successful hair and beauty professional.

With heartfelt wishes for your success,

Ebru Sak

PART ONE

Your First Moves

Name Your Baby

Choosing a name for your freelance business is an important step in establishing your brand identity. I've outlined some tips for you to help select a name and turn it into a compelling brand.

BE MEMORABLE AND UNIQUE

When selecting a name for your business, it's crucial to choose one that sets you apart from competitors and resonates with your audience. A name that stands out and is easy to remember can be a powerful asset in building brand recognition and attracting customers.

Avoiding generic or overly common names is important because you want your business to be distinctive and memorable. If your business name blends in with others in the industry, it can be challenging for customers to differentiate you from competitors. Instead, aim for a name that captures attention and leaves a lasting impression on those who come across it.

A distinctive name can help your business carve out its own identity and create a strong brand presence in the market. It should reflect your values, mission, and personality, resonating with your target audience and making them curious to learn more about what you offer.

By choosing a name that stands out and is easy to remember, you're laying a solid foundation for building brand awareness and loyalty, ultimately contributing to the success and longevity of your business.

CONSIDER RELEVANCE

When naming your business, it's essential to ensure the name reflects the nature of your business and the services you offer. Incorporating keywords related to hair, beauty, style, or the specific services you provide can effectively communicate the business in which you specialise.

By including relevant keywords in your business name, you're providing potential customers with valuable information at a glance. For example, if you operate a hair salon, using words like "hair", "salon", "styling" or specific services like "colouring" or "cuts" in your business name can immediately convey to customers what you offer.

This clarity is especially important in attracting your target audience. When people are searching for services in your industry, they often use keywords related to what they need. Having those keywords incorporated into your business name can increase the likelihood of your business appearing in search results and catching the attention of potential customers.

A name that clearly indicates your area of expertise can also help you stand out from competitors and establish credibility in your field.

KEEP IT SIMPLE

Select a name that rolls off the tongue effortlessly, is a breeze to spell, and sticks in the memory like a cherished melody. Opting for simplicity not only fosters instant brand recognition but also encourages natural, word-of-mouth recommendations. Steer clear of convoluted or puzzling names that could impede people from sharing your business with friends or family. After all, a name that's easy to say, spell, and remember is like a warm invitation, welcoming others to join in and be a part of your journey.

RESEARCH AVAILABILITY

Before finalising a name, research its availability. Check for domain name availability for your website and ensure there are no trademark conflicts. It's essential to have a name you can use consistently across all platforms without legal complications.

TEST IT OUT

Share potential names with friends, family, or members of your target market to gauge their reactions. Seek feedback on how the name resonates with them, the associations they make, and if it conveys the desired image for your service offerings.

BUILD A BRAND IDENTITY

Once you have chosen a name, it's time to develop your brand identity. Design a logo, choose a colour scheme, and create consistent visual elements that reflect the personality of your business. These elements will be crucial in establishing your brand and creating recognition in the market.

You have the option to shape your brand identity, craft a compelling logo, and curate a captivating colour palette using user-friendly platforms like Canva. This route offers a cost-effective approach, conserving your financial resources while allowing you to manifest your creative vision.

Alternatively, you can opt for a professional route by enlisting the expertise of a seasoned graphic designer. This investment will yield a bespoke style that harmonises seamlessly with your brand's essence.

Whether you embark on a solo design adventure or partner with a graphic virtuoso, the aim remains consistent: to forge a brand identity that is a true reflection of your freelance business. Your visual identity is more than just aesthetics; it is a language that speaks to your audience, conveying the values and character that set you apart.

CONSISTENCY IS KEY

Consistency in branding across all communication channels is crucial for establishing a strong and memorable business identity.

When you consistently use your business name, logo, and visual elements across various communication channels such as your website, social media profiles, and promotional materials, you're essentially reinforcing your brand identity in the minds of your audience.

Firstly, your business name serves as the primary identifier of your brand. By using it consistently across all platforms, you ensure that customers can easily recognise and remember your brand, regardless of where they encounter it.

Secondly, your logo is a visual representation of your brand and plays a significant role in brand recognition. When you use your logo consistently across different channels, it becomes synonymous with your business, making it easier for customers to associate it with your products and/or services.

In addition to your business name and logo, other visual elements such as colour schemes, typography, and imagery also contribute to your brand identity. By maintaining consistency in these visual elements across all communication channels, you create a cohesive and unified brand image that resonates with your audience.

Consistency in branding not only helps in immediate recognition but also fosters trust and credibility. When customers see a consistent brand presence across various platforms, it conveys professionalism and reliability, which can positively influence their perception of your business. It communicates a sense of stability and coherence, making it easier for customers to understand what your brand stands for and what they can expect from your products and/or services.

DELIVER ON YOUR PROMISES

Let's delve deeper into the importance of the relationship between your business name, brand, and customer experiences.

Your business name is the initial introduction to your brand, but it's the experiences you offer to your clients that truly shape how your business is perceived. Every interaction a customer has with your business—from the first point of contact to the service provided and even follow-up communication—contributes to their overall impression and perception of your brand.

Delivering exceptional service is key to creating positive experiences that leave a lasting impact on your clients. This involves not only meeting but exceeding their expectations at every touchpoint. Whether it's through the quality of your services, your professionalism, or the attentiveness to their needs, striving for excellence in every aspect of your business helps to create memorable experiences that customers will associate with your brand.

Maintaining a warm welcome is essential for fostering a sense of connection and rapport with your clients. A friendly and inviting atmosphere can make clients feel valued and appreciated, setting the tone for a positive experience from the moment they sit in front of the mirror.

Exceeding customer expectations is another crucial element in building a strong brand reputation. By going above and beyond to surprise and delight your clients, you not only leave a positive impression but also create loyal advocates who will enthusiastically recommend your business to others.

Positive experiences with your business will gradually build brand equity, associating your business name with quality, reliability, and excellence in the minds of your clients. This, in turn, strengthens your brand reputation and sets you apart from competitors in the hair and beauty industry.

It's important to recognise that building a brand is a long-term process that requires consistent effort and dedication. Choosing a name is just the beginning; it's the experiences you provide and the relationships you build with your clients that ultimately define your brand identity and reputation.

By delivering exceptional service, maintaining a warm welcome, and consistently exceeding customer expectations, you can create positive experiences that associate your business name with quality and build a strong brand reputation in the hair and beauty industry. Remember, building a brand takes time and careful consideration, but it's an opportunity to make a memorable and impactful presence in the industry.

CREATING MAGIC

There's something truly magical about working with hair. It's more than just a job; it's a passion that ignites my soul. I find immense joy in witnessing the transformation of women as they leave my salon with a newfound confidence, their steps light and their spirits lifted.

Over the years, I've come to understand that a visit to the hairdresser isn't merely about trimming split ends or adding a splash of colour, it's a deeply personal journey. Our hair is intricately woven into our identity; it reflects our innermost thoughts and feelings. When our locks refuse to cooperate, it's as if a part of ourselves is out of sync, leaving us feeling uneasy and insecure. We yearn for the effortless beauty we see in others, often struggling to replicate it ourselves. But there's a profound emotional connection intertwined with each snip of the scissors and stroke of the brush. As hairdressers, we become not just stylists but confidants and caretakers of our clients' emotions. We listen, we empathise, and we nurture, creating a safe space where they can unwind and be themselves.

To Start Things Off

Welcome to the exciting journey of Independent Hair and Beauty Freelancing. Renting space in a salon gives you the freedom to showcase your talents, build your client base, create a successful and lucrative independent freelance business in this fashion-driven, dynamic industry. Before you dive headfirst into this exhilarating journey, let's make sure you have all the essentials covered. After all, a strong foundation is the key to success.

EMBRACE YOUR INNER LEGAL EAGLE

Nobody wants to tangle with legal troubles or deal with financial fiascos. That's why understanding legal compliance and financial management is crucial. By taking the time to register your business name and secure your Australian Business Number (ABN), you're ensuring a smooth and worry-free journey. Stay on top of your income, expenses, and taxation obligations like a seasoned pro, and you'll be able to focus on what you do best – making your clients look and feel fabulous.

CRAFTING YOUR UNIQUE IDENTITY – REGISTERING THE NAME OF YOUR BUSINESS

Follow these steps to apply for a business name in Australia:

- **Research and Check Availability** – Before applying for a business name, conduct thorough research to ensure the name you desire is not already registered—or too similar—to an existing business name. You can use the Australian Securities and Investments Commission's (ASIC) business name search tool to check availability at **www.namecorp.com.au**

- **Create an ASIC Connect Account** – Visit the ASIC Connect website **www.connectonline.asic.gov.au** and create an account if you don't already have one. This account will allow you to register and manage your business name registration and other ASIC services.

- **Complete the Application** – Log in to your ASIC Connect account and select "Register a Business Name" from the menu. Fill in the required information, including your proposed business name, business structure (e.g., sole trader, partnership, company), and contact details.

- **Pay the Fee** – There is a registration fee associated with applying for a business name in Australia. The fee structure varies depending on the duration of registration (1 year or 3 years). You can make the payment online using a credit card or through other available payment methods.

- **Review and Submit** – Review the information you provided, ensuring accuracy and completeness. Submit the application through the ASIC Connect portal.

- **Wait for Confirmation** – Once you've submitted the application and made the payment, ASIC will process your application. If the business name registration is approved, you will receive a confirmation and the registered business name details will appear on the ASIC business names register.

It's important to note that registering a business name only provides the right to use that name. It does not provide exclusive ownership or trademark rights. If you require trademark protection, you should consider applying for a separate trademark registration through IP Australia at **www.ipaustralia.gov.au**

Remember to comply with any ongoing obligations such as renewing your business name registration within the specified timeframe and updating your details with ASIC if there are any changes. Mark the renewal date in your calendar and set a reminder to avoid the lapse of your business name.

For more detailed information and guidance, you can visit the ASIC website, **www.asic.gov.au** or seek professional advice from a business advisor or accountant.

GETTING AN AUSTRALIAN BUSINESS NUMBER (ABN)

Here are some reasons why obtaining an ABN serves the business owner:

Legitimacy and Professionalism

Having an ABN lends credibility to your business and demonstrates that you are a registered entity. It showcases professionalism and trustworthiness to potential clients and suppliers.

Taxation and Compliance

An ABN is a prerequisite for managing your business's tax obligations effectively. It allows you to register for Goods And Services Tax (GST) if your annual turnover exceeds the threshold, enabling you to collect and remit GST to the Australian Taxation Office (ATO).

Claiming Business-Related Expenses

With an ABN, you can claim business-related expenses, including purchases of goods and services, as tax deductions. This helps reduce your taxable income, potentially lowering your overall tax liability.

Access to Government Benefits and Support

Some government grants, subsidies, and support programs require businesses to have an ABN. By obtaining an ABN, you become eligible to access these valuable resources, which can assist in funding and growing your business.

Business Bank Account, Merchant Account and EFTPOS

Having an ABN is typically required to open a business bank account, merchant account, and obtain an EFTPOS machine. Here's a brief explanation of each requirement:

- **Business Bank Account** – Most banks in Australia require a valid ABN to open a business bank account. An ABN serves as a unique identifier for your business and is often a mandatory requirement to establish a business banking relationship. It helps ensure the account is associated with a legitimate business entity.

- **Merchant Account** – A merchant account enables businesses to accept payments from customers through credit card or debit card transactions. To set up a merchant account with a payment service provider or bank, you will generally need an ABN. The ABN verifies your business's identity and legitimacy when processing electronic payments.

- **EFTPOS Machine** – An Electronic Funds Transfer at Point of Sale (EFTPOS) machine allows businesses to accept card payments from customers at the point of sale. Many providers of EFTPOS services require an ABN to establish an account and lease or purchase an EFTPOS machine. The ABN is used to link the EFTPOS service to your business entity.

While an ABN is commonly required for these financial services, it's essential to note that specific requirements may vary among banks and payment service providers. It's recommended to contact the respective institution or provider you wish to engage with to understand their specific requirements and procedures for opening accounts and obtaining EFTPOS services. Some financial institutions may have additional requirements, such as business registration documents or identification proofs, to complete the account opening process.

To Obtain an Australian Business Number (ABN) in Australia

- **Gather Required Information** – Prepare the necessary information and documents for the application process. This may include your personal details (name, date of birth, address), business details (name, address, structure), and information about your business activities.

- **Choose the Application Method** – There are a few ways to apply for an ABN:

    a. *Online Application:* The fastest and most convenient method is to apply online through the Australian Business Register (ABR) website. This option is available 24/7.

    Visit the ABR website, **www.abr.gov.au** and select the option to apply for an ABN. Follow the prompts and provide the required information. Complete the application form, including details about your business structure, activities, and other relevant information. Double-check all the information before submitting the application.

b. *Registered Tax Agent or Business Activity Statement Agent:* If you prefer assistance with the application, you can engage a registered tax agent or business activity statement (BAS) agent to apply on your behalf.

c. *Registered Tax Agent or BAS Agent:* If you engage a registered tax agent or BAS agent, they will guide you through the application process, gather the necessary information, and submit the application on your behalf.

d. *Paper Application:* A paper application (Form NAT 2939) can be submitted by mail, but it generally takes longer to process compared to online applications.

e. *Paper Application:* If you choose the paper application method, download the Form NAT 2939 from the ABR website or obtain it from an Australian Taxation Office (ATO) shopfront. Fill in the form with the required details and mail it to the address provided on the form.

Once you submit the application, the processing time may vary. If your application is successful, you will receive an ABN and it will be recorded on the Australian Business Register. You will typically receive the ABN confirmation notice via email or mail.

Remember to keep your ABN details up to date and inform the ABR of any changes in your business structure, contact information, or business activities.

It's important to note that obtaining an ABN is free of charge. Be cautious of third-party services that may charge a fee for ABN applications. For further assistance or clarification, you can visit the ABR website, **www.abr.gov.au** or contact the Australian Taxation Office **www.ato.gov.au**

Freelance Insurance

As a freelance hair and beauty practitioner, it's important to have insurance coverage for several reasons. Here are some of the key points as to why it's important for a freelance hair and beauty professional to be insured:

Liability Coverage

Hair and beauty practitioners use tools and chemicals that can potentially cause harm or injury to clients. If a client is injured or suffers damage to their hair, skin and/or body as a result of your services, liability insurance can provide coverage for legal fees and damages.

Protection For Your Equipment

Hair and beauty equipment can be expensive and replacing it can be a financial burden if it's stolen, damaged, or lost. Insurance coverage can provide protection for your equipment, allowing you to replace or repair it quickly and easily.

Professional Indemnity Coverage

If a client is unhappy with your services or claims that you've made a mistake, professional indemnity insurance can protect you against any claims made against you.

Peace Of Mind

As a freelance hair and beauty practitioner, you're responsible for your own business and reputation. Having insurance coverage can provide you with peace of mind, knowing that you have protection in case something goes wrong.

Compliance With Legal Requirements

In some areas, having insurance coverage is a legal requirement for freelance hair and beauty practitioners. This means that if you're not insured, you could be subject to legal penalties or fines. It is beneficial to explore different options when seeking hair and beauty freelance insurance since each insurance company has its unique terms, conditions, and pricing guidelines.

Another option is to engage a broker who can handle the research on your behalf, although they will charge a commission for their services. Opting for a broker can be advantageous, allowing you to focus on your strengths while considering the value of time and using it wisely.

For all my insurance needs, I have relied on the expertise of a broker, **WKK Insurance Advisors.** Dealing with colossal insurance companies can be a daunting task, with their complicated processes and multiple departments to navigate in case of a claim. However, having a single broker in my corner alleviates that stress. I have complete confidence that my broker is advocating for me, diligently searching for the best insurer tailored to my requirements, and ensuring seamless claims handling if the need arises. The broker fee is unquestionably worthwhile as it grants me invaluable peace of mind. These small yet significant aspects of running a small business enable me to stay focused on what truly matters – building a thriving enterprise that paves the way to financial independence.

You can find the contact details to **WKK Insurance Advisors** at the back end of this guide in **My Little Gold Book of Contacts.** Ask for Jamie Keys, and mention my name. You will be looked after.

In summary, having insurance coverage as a freelance hair and beauty practitioner is important for protecting yourself, your clients, and your business. It provides coverage for liability, equipment, professional indemnity, and can give you peace of mind knowing that you're covered in case something goes wrong. It's important to take the time to research different insurance options and find the right coverage for your business.

Streamlining Your Business

Welcome to the world of independent hair and beauty freelancing, where managing your business with efficiency is the key to success. As a solo flyer, you have the freedom to chart your own course, and one tool that can significantly simplify your operations is online appointment software. Let's dive into why embracing this technology is a game-changer for independent hair and beauty professionals like yourself.

Seamless Appointment Booking

Kiss goodbye to the days of manual appointment books and endless phone calls. With online appointment software, you can offer your clients a seamless booking experience.

They can easily schedule appointments at their convenience from anywhere in the world. No more back-and-forth communication to find suitable time slots.

It's time-saving for both you and your clients, ensuring a smoother booking process.

Efficient Reminders and Notifications

Keeping your clients informed and reducing no-shows is essential for a thriving freelance business. Online appointment software comes to the rescue with automated reminders and notifications. Whether it's a confirmation email after booking, a friendly text reminder the day before their appointment, or updates about any changes, these timely messages ensure your clients arrive on time and well-prepared for their services.

Effective Communication and Updates

Maintaining open lines of communication is crucial for freelancers. Luckily, online appointment software simplifies this process by allowing you to effortlessly email clients with updates. Whether you have special offers, new services, or important announcements, a few clicks is all it takes to reach your entire client base.

Stay engaged and keep them in the loop about your business happenings.

Comprehensive Client Database

Providing personalised services requires organised client information. Say hello to a cloud-based online appointment software. It holds valuable client records, service instructions, and even custom-blend colour formulas. No more rummaging through stacks of paper or searching for scattered digital files. Everything you need is easily accessible and securely stored in one convenient place.

Time Management and Efficiency

Freelancers often juggle multiple tasks and appointments, so efficient time management is a must. Online appointment software empowers you to optimise your schedule, avoiding double-bookings and maximising productivity. With a quick glance at your digital calendar, you can see your availability and plan your day effectively. Maintain a balanced workload and bid farewell to scheduling conflicts.

Client Satisfaction and Professionalism

By utilising online appointment software, you demonstrate a high level of professionalism and commitment to exceptional client service. The ease of booking, timely reminders, and clear communication contribute to an overall positive client experience. Clients appreciate the convenience and reliability, building trust and encouraging repeat business.

SAM Australiapos, **www.australiapos.com.au** is my choice for salon software, and it's not without good reason. This incredible platform seamlessly fulfills all my business needs, offering a wide range of essential features including online booking, SMS reminders, powerful marketing tools, and efficient stock control. What's even more impressive is their exceptional customer support, always readily available to assist me whenever I need. Plus, the fact they are based right here in Australia gives me peace of mind, knowing that I have local support tailored to the unique needs of my salon business. With SAM Australiapos by my side, I can confidently manage and grow my freelance business with ease.

From simplifying booking processes and enhancing communication to maintaining a comprehensive client database, these tools empower you to streamline your operations, save time, and deliver a top-notch client experience. Embrace the advantages of online appointment software and watch your freelance business flourish with efficiency and professionalism. Remember, investing in the right tools can help propel your business forward and set you apart in a competitive market.

Customer Payment System

Let's talk about the not-so-glamorous but oh-so-important world of payments. Yes, I know, handling cash and swiping cards may not be as exciting as creating stunning hairstyles or flawless makeup looks but trust me, having your own payment system—like a fancy EFTPOS machine—can bring some serious perks and make your life a whole lot easier. Let's dive in and discover the benefits of embracing convenience!

Giving Your Clients Payment Power

We live in a world where everyone wants choices, even when it comes to paying for their hair and beauty services. By having your own payment system, you become the superhero of convenience, offering options galore. Credit card? Sure thing! EFTPOS? You got it! Cold, hard cash? Oh yeah, we've got that covered too!

Ensuring Secure Transactions

Having your own payment system provides an added layer of security for both you and your clients. With a trusted payment machine, credit card and EFTPOS, transactions are processed securely, protecting sensitive financial information.

This instils confidence in your clients, assuring them their payments are safe and that you prioritise their privacy and security.

Turning Number Crunching into Fun Munching

Accounting and record-keeping might sound as thrilling as watching paint dry, but fear not. Your personal payment system is here to rescue you from the abyss of spreadsheets and number nightmares. Thanks to your trusty machine, payments magically appear in your designated account, making bookkeeping a breeze. No more late-night sessions with calculators and stress-induced coffee runs.

PayID

PayID is a payment system that allows individuals and businesses to link their bank account to a unique identifier, such as a phone number or email address. It is primarily used in Australia, and it aims to simplify and streamline the payment process by eliminating the need to share bank account details. For small businesses, PayID can be a convenient and user-friendly payment option for customers. Here are a few reasons why it can be beneficial:

- **Seamless Transaction** – PayID allows for faster and more seamless transactions. Customers can make payments directly from their bank accounts without the need for third-party apps or additional steps.

- **Enhanced Security** – PayID employs robust security measures to protect sensitive information. When customers make payments using PayID, their bank details are not shared with the recipient, reducing the risk of potential data breaches or fraud.

- **Compatibility** – PayID is supported by numerous banks and financial institutions in Australia, making it widely accessible for both businesses and customers. This ensures the payment option is available to a broad range of users.

However, it's important to consider a few factors before implementing PayID for your business such as:

- **Customer Awareness** – Since PayID is relatively new, some customers may not be familiar with the concept or how to use it. It's essential to provide clear instructions and educate your customers about the payment method to ensure a smooth transition.

- **Payment Limitations** – PayID has certain transaction limits imposed by banks, which may vary depending on the financial institution and account type. Make sure to understand these limitations and communicate them to your customers to avoid any payment issues.

In the fast-paced world of independent hair and beauty freelancing, embracing your own payment system offers a range of benefits. From empowering client choice and streamlining the payment process to ensuring secure transactions and simplifying accounting, having an EFTPOS machine or similar payment system can enhance convenience, professionalism, and overall business efficiency.

PETRUS THE ARTIST

And then there is Petrus, a charming Dutch man with a creative flair for watercolour art. In his downtime, he paints whimsical and wonderful scenes of animals, people, and nature. His priceless pieces are never for sale; instead, he gifts them to those who matter to him. I am privileged to own two of Petrus's artworks, which serve as cherished monuments in my home. They symbolise that I am not just a hairdresser but also a friend who shares stories and connects with people from all walks of life. For me, the human connection is the most rewarding part of what I do.

PART TWO

Embarking on Your Path

Finding the Perfect Salon Space

As an independent hair and beauty freelancer, finding the right salon space from which to work is a crucial step towards establishing and growing your business. The salon you choose can greatly impact your success, productivity, and overall client experience. Here are some essential factors to consider when searching for the perfect salon space that aligns with your needs and enhances your freelance journey.

Before approaching any salon, invest time in thorough research to identify salons that align with your brand and professional goals. Look for salons that specialise in services complementary to your own. Consider factors such as their reputation, clientele, and overall atmosphere. Seek a salon where your unique talents and services will seamlessly blend, creating a harmonious and collaborative environment.

Location, Location, Location

The first and foremost aspect to consider is the location of the salon. Ideally, you'll want to find a salon that is easily accessible to your target clientele. Look for a location that is conveniently located, whether it's in a bustling city centre, a trendy neighbourhood, or near residential areas with high foot traffic. Consider factors such as parking availability, public transportation options, and the overall ambiance of the surrounding area.

Amenities and Facilities

Assess the amenities and facilities provided by potential salon spaces. Look for a salon that offers the necessary equipment and tools for your hair and beauty services. Consider the availability of comfortable seating, well-lit workstations, ample storage space for your supplies, and functional washbasins. Additionally, check if the salon has proper ventilation and meets all safety and hygiene standards.

Atmosphere and Ambience

The atmosphere and ambience of a salon play a significant role in creating a positive experience for your clients. Visit prospective salons and pay attention to the overall vibe and aesthetics. Does it align with your brand and the type of clients you want to attract? Consider factors such as decor, lighting, music, and overall cleanliness. A welcoming and visually appealing salon can enhance your clients' satisfaction and loyalty.

Rental Terms and Costs

Carefully review the rental terms and costs associated with each salon space. Evaluate the financial feasibility and ensure it aligns with your budget. Consider factors such as daily, weekly, or monthly rent and any additional expenses of which you need to be aware. It's essential to have a clear understanding of the financial commitment required and ensure it aligns with your business goals.

Determining the ideal rates for renting salon space can be

quite the conundrum. It all boils down to finding the perfect balance between location, space, and the extra perks. One way to approach it is by crunching the numbers and estimating your daily revenue. Then, consider allocating around 10 to 20% of that as a reasonable rental rate. Remember, ultimately, the decision is in your hands. You're the boss here!

Flexibility and Freedom

As a freelancer, it's crucial to assess the level of flexibility and freedom you'll have within the salon space. Determine if the salon allows you to set your own schedule, work with your preferred products, and maintain your personal brand identity. Discuss any potential restrictions or limitations with the salon owner or manager to ensure it aligns with your vision and goals.

Networking and Collaboration Opportunities

Consider the potential for networking and collaboration within the salon space. Some salons host events, workshops, or have a community of freelancers working together. This can provide valuable opportunities to expand your professional network, learn from others in the industry, and potentially collaborate on projects such as groups for bridal parties and bridal showers. Building connections within the salon can open doors to new clients and collaborations, boosting your freelance career.

Finding the right salon space as a hair and beauty freelancer is a crucial step towards creating a successful and thriving business.

Dress for Success

SLAYING THE HAIR AND BEAUTY GAME WITH STYLE

Let's talk about the power of a killer uniform. It's not just about the talent and skills you bring to the table; it's about looking the part too! So, buckle up and get ready to discover why a consistent and on-brand uniform is the secret weapon to conquer the industry in style.

Unleash Your Brand Identity

You're not just a hair and beauty pro, you're a walking brand. Your brand identity is like your signature scent, it sets you apart from the crowd. And guess what? Your uniform plays a starring role in this glamorous show. By designing a uniform that reflects your brand's vibe, colours, and logo, you'll have clients swooning over your impeccable style while reinforcing your professional image. It's like wearing a billboard that screams: "I'm fabulous and I know it!"

Build Client Confidence (and a Fan Club)

Consistency is the key to unlocking client love and loyalty. When you rock your brand-aligned uniform day in and day out, clients will know they can count on you. It's like being their hair and beauty superhero, ready to save the day with your magical skills.

Own Your Professional Image

As a hair and beauty freelancer, you are the CEO of your own glam empire, and CEOs always dress to impress! Your uniform is your superhero cape, instantly transforming you into a beacon of professionalism and dedication. It shows clients that you mean business, that you're meticulous about the details, and you're a master of your craft. When you look like a boss, clients trust you like a boss.

The impact of a well-designed and consistently-worn uniform cannot be underestimated in the world of hair and beauty freelancing. By aligning your uniform with your brand identity, you create a powerful visual representation of your professionalism, build client confidence and enhance the overall client experience. Embrace the power of a uniform that complements your brand and watch as it becomes an integral part of your success in this dynamic industry.

THE MAGIC

Working with hair isn't just a job, it's a passion that ignites my soul. Witnessing the transformation of women leaving my salon with newfound confidence brings me immense joy. Beyond trimming split ends or adding colour, I've realized that a salon visit is a deeply personal journey, intricately tied to identity. Our locks reflect our innermost thoughts and feelings, and as hairdressers, we become confidants and caretakers of our clients' emotions. With each snip of the scissors and stroke of the brush, we nurture a profound emotional connection, creating a safe space for our clients to unwind and be themselves.

Occupational Health and Safety Guidelines for Freelancers

Maintaining appropriate attire and following occupational health and safety guidelines are essential for independent hair and beauty professionals freelancing in salons. By adhering to these guidelines, you can ensure a safe and professional working environment. Please read and follow the recommendations outlined below.

Clothing

Wear clean, professional attire that reflects your personal style while maintaining a polished appearance. Avoid loose-fitting or excessively baggy clothing that may interfere with your work or pose safety risks. Consider wearing clothing made of breathable fabrics that provide comfort during long working hours. Choose clothing with pockets, aprons, or a tool belt to keep necessary tools and supplies easily accessible.

Footwear

Wear closed-toe shoes with non-slip soles to ensure stability and minimise the risk of slips or falls. Avoid high heels or open-toe shoes that may be unsafe or impractical for certain tasks. Select comfortable shoes that provide adequate support to minimize fatigue during long periods of standing.

Jewellery and Accessories

Minimise the use of jewellery, such as dangling earrings, bracelets, or rings, that may pose safety hazards or interfere with your work. Keep nails neatly trimmed and avoid excessively long or decorative nails that may hinder your ability to perform tasks.

Ergonomics

Maintain proper posture and body mechanics while performing treatments or working with clients to prevent strain or injury. Adjust the height of chairs, tables, and equipment to ensure ergonomic positioning that supports your comfort and reduces the risk of repetitive strain injuries (RSI). Take regular breaks and stretch to prevent muscle tension or stiffness.

Sanitation and Hygiene

Follow strict hygiene practices, including frequent handwashing and the use of hand sanitisers. Disinfect tools and equipment between clients to prevent the spread of bacteria, viruses, and infections. Keep your workstation clean and organised, removing clutter and promptly disposing of waste materials.

Chemical Safety

Use products and chemicals in accordance with manufacturer instructions, following recommended dilution ratios and safety precautions. Wear appropriate personal protective equipment (PPE), such as gloves and goggles, when handling chemicals that may be harmful or irritants. Ensure proper ventilation in the workspace to minimise exposure to fumes or airborne particles.

Electrical Safety

Inspect electrical cords and equipment regularly for any signs of damage, such as fraying or exposed wires. Avoid overloading electrical outlets and use surge protectors when necessary. Keep electrical cords and equipment away from water sources to prevent electrical hazards.

First Aid and Emergency Preparedness

Have a well-stocked first aid kit readily available and familiarise yourself with its contents and usage. Know the location of emergency exits, fire extinguishers, and other safety equipment within the salon. Familiarise yourself with emergency procedures, including evacuation plans, in case of an unexpected event.

Remember, these guidelines are intended to promote safety, professionalism, and client satisfaction. By following appropriate attire and occupational health and safety practices, you contribute to a positive work environment and ensure the well-being of both you and your clients.

Upholding Professionalism and Ethical Work Practices

In the ever-evolving world of hair and beauty freelancing, maintaining professionalism and ethical work practices is essential for success. Here, we explore the significance of embodying these principles and the positive impact they have on your career as an independent professional. By adhering to a code of conduct and ethical guidelines, you can create a respectful and satisfying work environment for both you and your clients.

Professionalism – Creating a Lasting Impression

Maintaining a polished and professional image is crucial in the hair and beauty industry. Your appearance speaks volumes about your commitment to excellence. Take pride in presenting yourself in a neat and clean manner, ensuring you make a positive first impression on your clients.

Punctuality is Key

Time is a valuable commodity for both you and your clients. Being punctual demonstrates respect for their schedules and shows that you value their time. Arrive promptly for appointments and honour the agreed-upon schedule, allowing for a smooth and efficient flow of services.

Respecting Salon Policies and Guidelines

When working in a shared space or renting a room in a salon, it's important to adhere to the established policies, procedures, and guidelines. By doing so, you contribute to a harmonious and cooperative environment that benefits everyone involved.

Client Care and Communication
– Building Trust and Loyalty

Your clients are at the heart of your business. Prioritise their satisfaction by delivering high-quality services and actively listening to their needs and preferences.

Clear and transparent communication regarding pricing, services, and any potential risks or limitations is essential for building trust and ensuring clients feel informed and confident in your expertise.

Keep in mind also to maintain a considerate boundary and respect their privacy. In my practice, I have a simple rule: I steer clear of discussions on politics and religion. These topics can be deeply personal, and everyone holds their own unique perspective. To put it humorously, I prefer to adopt a "Switzerland" approach, remaining neutral and impartial. By respecting the diverse views and beliefs of my clients, I create a comfortable and inclusive environment for all.

Hygiene and Sanitation – Safety First

Maintaining proper hygiene and sanitation practices is paramount in the hair and beauty industry. Regularly wash your hands, sanitise tools and equipment, and use clean or sanitised materials such as towels and capes. By following strict hygiene standards, you create a safe and comfortable environment for both you and your clients.

Confidentiality and Privacy – Trust and Respect

Respecting client confidentiality and privacy is a fundamental ethical obligation. Safeguard their personal information, including medical history and treatment records, and obtain consent before sharing any client-related information with third parties, including posts on social media. Complying with data protection and privacy regulations ensures that clients trust you with their sensitive information.

Continuous Professional Development – Stay Ahead of the Curve

The beauty industry is constantly evolving, and it's essential to stay updated with the latest trends, techniques, and safety practices. Invest in continuous education and training to enhance your skills and knowledge, ensuring you provide the highest level of service to your clients. Complying with relevant licensing and certification requirements adds credibility to your professional profile.

Ethical Business Practices – Integrity and Fairness

Maintain integrity in your business operations by practising ethical standards. Advertise your services truthfully and accurately, avoiding misleading claims. Respect intellectual property rights and refrain from unauthorised use or distribution of copyrighted materials. Engage in fair competition, focusing on your unique strengths rather than undermining others.

Creating a Supportive Environment – Collaboration and Growth

Fostering a supportive and collaborative atmosphere with fellow freelancers and salon staff creates a positive work environment. Share knowledge, experiences, and resources that can benefit others, contributing to the growth and success of the entire hair and beauty community.

By embracing professionalism and ethical work practices, you lay the foundation for a thriving freelance career in the hair and beauty industry. Upholding these standards ensures client satisfaction, builds trust, and fosters a positive work environment. By adhering to a code of conduct and ethical guidelines, you not only elevate your own reputation but also contribute to the overall excellence of the industry.

Upkeep Tools and Equipment

As an independent hair and beauty freelancer, in addition to delivering exceptional services, maintaining a professional image is crucial. One often overlooked aspect is the cleanliness, tidiness, and proper maintenance of your products, tools and equipment. Whether you're renting space in a salon or working on-the-go, the way you handle and present your tools can leave a lasting impression on clients and contribute to your overall reputation.

It's your responsibility to keep your products, tools and equipment clean, tidy, and in working condition, as well as neatly carting it in and out of salons when renting space.

Client Satisfaction and Safety

Clean and well-maintained equipment is essential for client satisfaction and safety. By regularly cleaning and sanitising your tools, you demonstrate professionalism and a commitment to maintaining high hygiene standards. Clients appreciate a clean and sanitised environment, which enhances their overall experience and builds trust in your services. Additionally, properly maintained equipment reduces the risk of accidents or damage during treatments, ensuring the safety and well-being of both you and your clients.

Professional Image

Your equipment reflects your professionalism and attention to detail. When clients observe you using clean, organised tools, it instils confidence in your expertise and the quality of your services. On the other hand, unkempt or malfunctioning equipment may raise doubts about your professionalism and competence. By investing time in keeping your equipment in pristine condition, you create a positive and lasting impression, strengthening your professional image and setting yourself apart from the competition.

Safety First – Securely Storing Sharp Tools for Peace of Mind

Keeping sharp tools safe and out of reach is of utmost importance to ensure both your safety and that of your clients. One effective method is to store such tools in a waistbelt or apron pocket. By securely placing sharp implements in designated compartments, you minimise the risk of accidental injury or damage. By maintaining a systematic approach to tool storage, you can work with confidence, knowing that your sharp tools are safely stowed and easily accessible when needed.

Extended Lifespan of Equipment

Regular maintenance and care significantly extend the lifespan of your equipment. Cleaning removes product build-up, preventing clogs or malfunctions. Proper storage and organisation reduce the risk of damage or loss. By implementing a maintenance routine, you can maximise the longevity of your tools, saving you money in the long run and ensuring you always have reliable equipment at your disposal.

Carting Around Your Equipment

When you are renting space in a salon, the way you cart your equipment in and out can make a difference. Neatly organising and transporting your tools not only showcases your professionalism but also demonstrates respect for the salon environment. I have discovered that utilising small suitcases typically used for boarding aircraft works wonders for me. Instead of straining myself with heavy lifting, I simply wheel it around effortlessly. Arriving and leaving the salon with a clean and tidy suitcase creates a positive impression on both salon staff and fellow freelancers.

Client Perceptions and Word-Of-Mouth

Clients notice the small details, including how you handle your equipment. A clean and organised setup shows that you value your work and prioritise their experience. Satisfied clients are more likely to share their positive experiences with others, leading to word-of-mouth recommendations and potential new business opportunities. On the other hand, negative experiences or perceptions due to neglected equipment can spread just as quickly, potentially harming your reputation and client base.

When renting space in salons, carting your equipment neatly highlights your professionalism and respect for the salon environment. Remember, the small details matter, and taking care of your equipment demonstrates your commitment to providing top-notch services and establishing a strong reputation in the industry.

So, embrace the importance of cleanliness, tidiness, and proper maintenance. Elevate your freelance journey by ensuring your equipment shines as brightly as your talent and passion!

CHRIS AND PIP THE LITTLE LAMB

Meet Chris, a shepherdess with a heart as tender as the lambs for which she cares. Amidst her regular salon appointments, her hair serves as a canvas for vibrant hues reflecting the vivid colours of her life. Through each visit, Chris shares poignant tales of her flock—of births under the open sky; some joyous, others heart-wrenching as mothers reject their young. Yet, Chris never turns away, offering solace and sustenance to the abandoned with tender hands and overflowing compassion. Amongst these stories, the bittersweet saga of Little Pip unfolds – a lamb whose broken leg casts a shadow over his once spirited demeanour. Chris's decision to alleviate his suffering is shared during a salon visit, tears blending with the wash of hair dye, illustrating her profound connection to both her flock and her own journey.

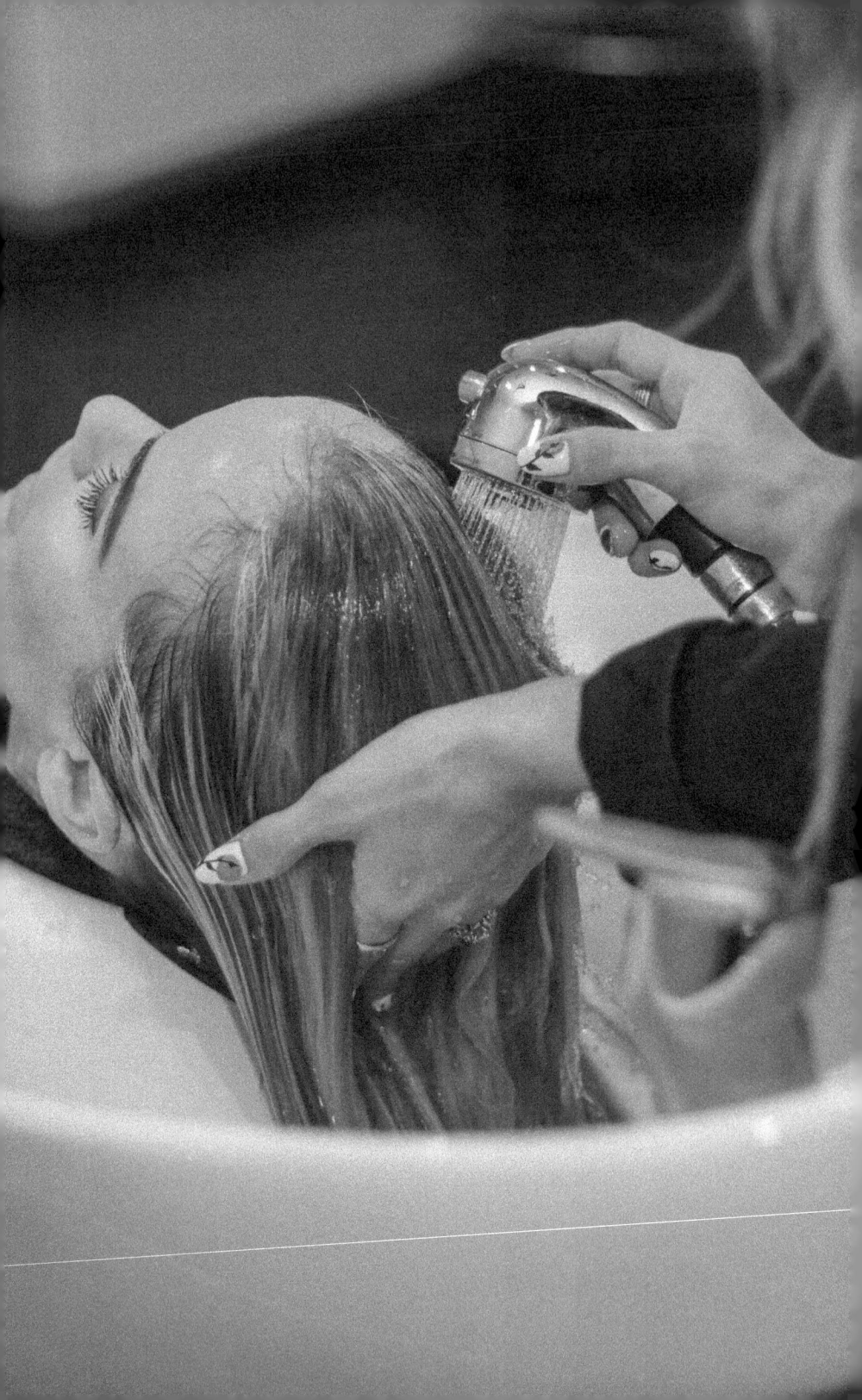

PART THREE

The Heart of
the Process

Fuelling Your Passion

Imagine the beauty of the sunrise, the melody of birdsong, and the invigorating energy that fills your being as you start your day. This is the essence of passion that fuels our journey in the realm of self-employment. Now, let's delve into the strategies that will help us nurture this passion and cultivate a harmonious atmosphere for our valued clients.

Embrace Active Listening

In the hustle and bustle of our profession, it's easy to get caught up in the rhythm of our own voices. However, as hair and beauty freelancers, it's essential to shift our focus from talking to listening. By actively listening to our clients' needs, desires, and concerns, we create a space where they feel heard and understood. This not only strengthens the client-professional relationship but also helps deliver an experience tailored to their individual preferences.

Leave the Weight Outside the Salon

We all have our own circus of challenges, but when you step into your magical salon realm, leave the heavy stuff at the door. Your clients come seeking refuge from the chaos of the outside world. They're here to escape, rejuvenate, and maybe even have a fabulous hair transformation. So, let's create a stress-free zone where unicorns roam free, happy vibes abound, and the only weight we carry is the blow dryer in our skilled hands.

Make the Client the Star and Roll Out the Red Carpet

When your clients strut through that salon door, it's showtime. They're not just looking for a quick trim; they're craving an experience fit for the runway. So, turn up the charm, sprinkle some magic dust, and make them feel like the VIPs they truly are.

Nurture Your Passion

To keep the flame alive, we must nurture our own passion for the art of fashion, hair, and beauty. Take the time to engage in continuous learning, stay updated with the latest trends, and seek inspiration from various sources. Attend workshops, connect with fellow professionals, and explore new techniques. By constantly evolving and challenging ourselves, we not only enhance our skills but also reignite that spark within us.

Success and Mindset

Maintaining a positive outlook when facing our own personal challenges can be difficult; however, in a service-based business, your interactions with people can reveal your energy, even if you try to hide your struggles. That's why I find it crucial to prioritise my own well-being by immersing myself in the wisdom of empowered individuals who have mastered the art of happiness.

For me, building resilience starts with embracing a morning routine that sets the tone for the day. I rise early to have precious moments of solitude, allowing me to find my centre. One technique I find helpful is writing three pages of longhand, which helps me clear my mind and create a positive mindset to kickstart my day. Maintaining balanced energy levels is also essential, and I achieve this by nourishing my body with a well-rounded diet.

To fill my cup with inspiration, I turn to influential gurus like **Wayne Dyer, Lisa Nichols and Brene Brown,** whose words resonate deeply with me. Additionally, I delve into books by **Julia Cameron**, such as *The Artist's Way*, which provides me with a daily dose of motivation and creativity.

By prioritising my personal well-being and drawing wisdom from these sources, I can approach my work with a positive mindset, ensuring the energy I bring to each customer interaction is uplifting and genuine. After all, when we take care of ourselves, we can better serve those who rely on us.

As independent freelance hair and beauty professionals, we have the power to create an extraordinary experience for our clients. By waking each morning with passion and a bounce in our step, and by embracing active listening and leaving our own burdens outside the salon, we cultivate an environment where clients find harmony and happiness. Remember, it's not just about the transaction; it's about creating a fabulous journey for our clients. So, let your passion shine, and let's make every day a celebration of creativity, skill, and exceptional client experiences.

Your Customer Avatar

Get ready to dive into the wild world of customer avatars! It's like being a detective but instead of solving crimes, we're unravelling the mysteries of our ideal clients. Here, we'll explore how defining your customer avatar is the secret sauce to success in the hair and beauty industry.

I can't stress enough the importance of pinpointing your ultimate superstar customer and the service you absolutely love doing. This magical combo will transform you into a true authority and ruler in your specialised realm, making you a magnet for the perfect customers.

I made the goof of trying to be a jack-of-all-trades, catering to everyone and their cousin, and boy, did I pay the price! Lost customers faster than a dropped curling iron. It was stress city, my friend. So, take my advice and embrace the power of saying "no". Focus your energy on the clients you adore, and watch your career flourish like a freshly-styled bouffant!

Defining Your Customer Avatar

When you're aware of your strengths and find joy in what you're passionate about, identifying your ideal customer avatar becomes a straightforward task. For instance, if you have a passion for hair extensions, you can discern who your most suitable customers are based on factors such as their age, gender or non-binary, lifestyle, preferences, and even the challenges they face. By constructing this thorough profile, you'll attain a deep comprehension of your target audience, effectively crafting a roadmap that guides you to the hearts and wallets of your perfect clients.

Tailoring Services to Woo Your Dream Clients

Now that you've found your perfect match, it's time to sweep them off their feet with tailor-made services. Think of it as creating a bespoke outfit for each client. Whether it's offering specialised hair treatments, beauty services for specific skin types, or personalised consultations, customising your services shows that you understand their unique needs. You'll be the hair and beauty expert they can't resist!

Pricing Strategies

Ah, pricing, the dance of love between your business and your customers' wallets. With your customer avatar in mind, it's time to set your prices strategically. Take into account their purchasing power, preferences, and how they perceive value. It's like finding that sweet spot between making them feel like a million bucks and keeping your business profitable. Get those numbers to do a little dance that leaves everyone happy!

Staying Focused – Resist the Temptation to be Everything to Everyone

Listen up, my friend, it's time to resist the siren call of trying to please everyone. I know it's tempting to cater to a wider audience but staying focused on your chosen demographic is the secret to success. By staying true to your customer avatar, you position yourself as the expert in your specialised services. Think of it as being the go-to hairstylist or beauty guru for a specific tribe. Trust me, staying focused will make you a legend in your niche!

Marketing Magic – Cast Your Spell on Your Ideal Clients

Now that you've cracked the code of your customer avatar, it's time to work your marketing magic. Craft messages that speak directly to your ideal clients, like a secret language only they understand. From social media campaigns that make their hearts skip a beat to personalised email marketing that feels like a love letter, your marketing efforts will hit the bullseye. Show them how your services address their specific needs and desires then watch them flock to your doorstep!

So, my artistic maestro, defining your customer avatar is like having a secret weapon in your arsenal. By understanding their wants, needs, and deepest desires, you can tailor your services, pricing, and marketing efforts to attract and retain your dream clients. Stay focused, be strategic, and get ready to witness your business flourish with a loyal and satisfied client base. It's time to unleash your inner customer whisperer and conquer the hair and beauty world one fabulous client at a time!

The Ripple Effect of Marketing

In the world of hair and beauty services, generating new clients is a constant goal for independent professionals. One of the most effective ways to achieve this is by leveraging the power of word-of-mouth recommendations from your existing clients. Additionally, utilising email marketing to engage with and reward your loyal client base can further amplify your reach. In this chapter, we explore the strategies of encouraging word-of-mouth referrals and leveraging email marketing for special occasions, such as birthdays. By implementing these techniques, you can create a ripple effect of new client acquisition, loyalty, and business growth.

Nurturing Word-of-Mouth Referrals

Word-of-mouth referrals are invaluable for expanding your client base. Encourage your existing clients to recommend your services to their friends, family, and colleagues. One effective way to incentivise this behaviour is by implementing a referral program. Reward your existing clients with a gift voucher or a special discount on their next visit for every successful referral they bring in. This not only motivates your clients to share their positive experiences but also gives them a tangible benefit, creating a win-win situation.

Utilising Email Marketing for Client Engagement

Email marketing is a valuable tool for staying connected with your existing clients and nurturing those relationships. Get your clients' permission to receive emails from you with regular updates, exclusive offers, and personalised content.

Additionally, leverage special occasions such as birthdays to send personalised greetings and exclusive birthday offers. This thoughtful gesture not only strengthens the bond with your clients but also encourages them to book appointments and spread the word about your services.

Crafting Compelling Email Campaigns

Tailor your messages to resonate with their needs and preferences. Include information about new services, promotions, or seasonal offers that may be of interest to them. Additionally, consider incorporating personalised recommendations based on their previous visits and preferences. By delivering valuable and personalised content, you enhance client engagement and increase the likelihood of them sharing your messages with their network.

Google Reviews

Google testimonials are like having your own personal cheerleading squad on the internet! It's like getting others to do the happy dance for you and your amazing work. So, don't be shy, ask your customers to show off their moves by leaving a fantastic Google review. But hey, if you want to take it up a notch, why not serenade them with a friendly phone call, text, or email?

Now, we know that perfection is a tough act to pull off, and sometimes a customer may not be doing the happy dance. You can swoop in and save the day by offering them a chance to come back and rectify their hairdo. Trust me, it's the ultimate "avoid-a-bad-review" strategy.

Just remember, once a review hits the internet, it's like a virtual tattoo – hard to erase. So, let's keep those positive vibes flowing and make sure your customers' experiences are so great that they can't wait to shout about it from the digital rooftops.

Word-of-mouth recommendations and email marketing are two powerful tools for expanding your client base and fostering client loyalty. By encouraging word-of-mouth referrals through referral programs and providing incentives, you empower your existing clients to become brand advocates and generate new business for you.

Additionally, email marketing allows you to stay connected with your clients, nurturing those relationships and driving engagement.

Remember, happy clients are more likely to share their positive experiences, and by rewarding them for their loyalty and referrals, you encourage a ripple effect of new client acquisition. Leverage the power of word-of-mouth and email marketing to create a thriving community of satisfied clients who not only return to your salon but also become active promoters of your brand.

HAIR IS NOT EVERYTHING

Rebecca's teenage years were overshadowed by a deep internal struggle, manifested in the gradual loss of her hair. What began as a few strands falling out turned into a veil of insecurity, isolating her from the world. Behind her beanies, she longed for acceptance and understanding until her mother's loving intervention led her to my salon chair. There, amidst the bustling atmosphere, Rebecca found solace and hope. With each visit, I not only tended to her hair but nurtured her spirit, sharing stories of resilience and recommending books that guided my own journey of self-discovery. Through our interactions, Rebecca learned that true beauty comes from within, and as she left the salon, beanie-free and confident, she embraced her uniqueness and embarked on a journey of self-love and acceptance, knowing that greatness lies in embracing one's individuality.

Unleash Your Online Influence

In today's digital age, having a strong social media presence has become a necessity for hair and beauty independent freelancers. Social media platforms offer a unique and powerful opportunity to connect with clients, showcase your work, and build a strong personal brand. Here's why having a social media presence is essential.

Reach and Visibility

Social media platforms provide a vast audience reach, allowing you to highlight your skills and services to a large number of potential clients. With billions of active users, platforms like Facebook and Instagram enable you to connect with people near and far. By leveraging social media, you expand your visibility beyond the confines of your local area, increasing your chances of attracting new clients and expanding your business.

Building a Personal Brand

In the hair and beauty industry, personal branding plays a crucial role. Social media platforms offer you the opportunity to curate and showcase your unique brand identity. Through consistent and engaging content, you can establish yourself as an expert in your field, highlighting your skills, creativity, and unique style. This helps you differentiate yourself from competitors and allows potential clients to get to know and trust you before even making their first appointment with you.

Showcasing Your Portfolio

Social media acts as a virtual portfolio, allowing you to display your work in a visually appealing and easily accessible manner. Platforms like Instagram are particularly effective for sharing before-and-after transformations, intricate hairstyles, flawless makeup looks, or stunning nail art.

By regularly updating your social media with high-quality images and videos of your work, you create a visual narrative that captivates potential clients and demonstrates your expertise.

Engaging With Your Audience

Social media is all about building connections and engaging with your audience. It provides a direct line of communication between you and your clients. Through comments, direct messages, and even live video sessions, you can engage with your audience, answer their questions, provide beauty tips, and offer personalised recommendations. This interaction not only helps in building a loyal client base but also fosters a sense of community around your brand.

Social Proof and Testimonials

Social media allows clients to share their experiences with your services in the form of reviews, comments, and testimonials. Positive feedback and endorsements from satisfied clients act as social proof, influencing the decision-making process of potential clients. By encouraging clients to leave reviews and testimonials on your social media platforms, you build trust and credibility, making it easier for new clients to choose you over your competitors.

Staying Updated With Trends

The hair and beauty industry are constantly evolving, with new trends and techniques emerging regularly. Social media serves as a treasure trove of inspiration and information. By following industry experts, influencers, and brands on social media, you can stay updated with the latest trends, styles, and products. This knowledge allows you to offer cutting-edge services to your clients, positioning yourself as a knowledgeable and trend-savvy professional.

We all come from diverse backgrounds, and not all of us are naturally tech-savvy or have the patience to navigate social media platforms and post on them regularly. If you find yourself in this situation, don't worry! There's a solution that can help your freelance business thrive in the digital world: outsourcing your social media management.

There are numerous businesses out there specialising in managing social media portfolios for small businesses, and they often offer their services at an affordable price so you can have a consistent social media presence without having to struggle through it on your own.

Here's why it's worth considering outsourcing your social media management:

Time-Saving

Running a small business involves numerous responsibilities, and managing social media can be time-consuming. Outsourcing this task allows you to focus on other core aspects of your business, such as product development, customer service, and growth strategies.

Consistency and Frequency

Maintaining a regular social media presence is crucial for building brand awareness and engaging with your audience. Social media management experts can create a content calendar, schedule posts in advance, and ensure your business has a consistent presence online.

Content Creation

Coming up with engaging and visually appealing content can be challenging, especially if you're not familiar with the latest trends or tools. Social media management services often provide content creation, including graphics, images, and videos, tailored to your brand's voice and target audience.

By outsourcing your social media management, you can enjoy the benefits of having a consistent and professional social media presence without the stress and learning curve. Remember, even if you can't dedicate time or lack expertise in this area, it's better to have a regular presence on social media platforms than none at all.

Having a social media presence is no longer a luxury but a necessity for hair and beauty independent freelancers. It enables you to reach a wider audience, build a strong personal brand, showcase your portfolio, engage with clients, and stay updated with industry trends.

Power of a Website

In today's digital age, having a strong online presence is crucial for businesses across all industries, including the hair and beauty sector. Small business hair and beauty freelancers, in particular, can significantly benefit from having a website that highlights their work, skills, operating hours, price list, services offered, and locations from which they work. By providing potential customers with a comprehensive view of their offerings, freelancers can build trust, attract new clients, and ultimately increase their bookings.

Visual Showcase of Skills and Expertise

One of the most compelling reasons for hair and beauty freelancers to have a website is to display their work and demonstrate their skills and expertise. High-quality images and testimonials can showcase their talent and creativity, giving potential customers a glimpse into the level of service they can expect. By providing visual proof of their abilities, freelancers can instil confidence in their potential clients, making them more likely to choose their services over competitors.

Information Accessibility

Customers appreciate transparency and readily available information. A website acts as a centralised hub where freelancers can provide detailed information about their services, pricing, operating hours, and the locations they serve. This accessibility empowers customers to make informed decisions without having to make numerous phone calls or send countless messages. They can easily browse the website and quickly gather all the essential information they need before deciding to book a freelancer.

Trust and Credibility

In an industry where trust is paramount, having a professional website establishes credibility and authenticity. A well-designed website with a polished appearance reflects professionalism and competence, allowing potential clients to feel confident in their choice of a hair or beauty freelancer. By investing in a website, freelancers show their commitment to their craft and their dedication to providing exceptional services, which helps to build trust with potential customers.

If you're interested in developing your own website and saving costs, there are various platforms available that offer user-friendly, drag-and-drop features for creating websites, such as **WIX** or **SQUARESPACE.** You can give it a try and experiment with these platforms for free before making any commitments. This allows you to familiarise yourself with the tools and explore the possibilities of designing your own website without any financial obligations.

After exploring various website building platforms, I made the decision to create my website using **WIX**. It is user-friendly and makes it perfect for someone like me with no technical background to create my very own website. I challenged myself to learn to create my own website and now I confidently handle updates, make changes, and upload products to my online store all on my own. If I can do it, anyone can! So, go ahead and give it a try. You'll be amazed at what you can accomplish.

Improved Customer Reach and Engagement

A website is a powerful tool for expanding the customer reach of hair and beauty freelancers. With an online presence, freelancers are no longer limited to local customers. A website enables them to attract clients from different locations, whether it's within the same city or even beyond. By optimising their website for search engines like Google and linking social media channels such as Instagram and Facebook, freelancers can increase their visibility and engage with a broader audience, leading to a higher chance of bookings and referrals.

Booking Convenience

A website simplifies the booking process for both the freelancer and the client. By incorporating an online Appointment and Booking System into your website, freelancers can provide a seamless experience for customers who can schedule appointments at their convenience, 24/7. This eliminates the need for back-and-forth communication and allows clients to secure their desired time slot without delay. The ease and convenience of online booking can give freelancers a competitive edge and enhance customer satisfaction.

In an increasingly digital world, small business hair and beauty freelancers must recognise the importance of establishing a strong online presence. Embracing technology and investing in a website is a wise decision that can elevate a hair and beauty freelancer's business in today's competitive market.

Adding Your Personal Touch

In the midst of a bustling and highly-competitive industry, it is essential to find ways to differentiate yourself from other service providers. One effective strategy is to incorporate a personal touch that leaves a lasting impression on your clients. This could manifest in various ways, such as the manner in which you greet them and bid them farewell, or even small gestures like offering assistance with their jackets. These personalised actions become your signature, setting you apart from the crowd.

Another way to infuse your personal touch into your freelancing business is by providing a selection of teas and coffees, accompanied by delicious biscuits. This thoughtful offering can create a warm and welcoming atmosphere for your clients. Whether they are visiting you for a brief 20-minute service or a luxurious three-hour session, the offering of herbal tea and coffee adds an extra touch of comfort and hospitality.

As a salon owner and a freelancer, I have made it a standard practice to offer a variety of herbal teas and coffee options to all my clients. To maintain consistency in every aspect of my service, I also ensure that I use the same brand of milk and biscuits. By selecting a specific brand and consistently offering it to my clients, I establish a familiar and comforting experience that aligns with my overall personal touch.

This attention to detail further reinforces my commitment to providing a consistently exceptional service and creates a sense of reliability and trust in my freelancing business. Furthermore, I personally accompany each client as they leave and ensure to open the door for them. These small gestures are an inherent part of who I am as a professional, and they reflect the high standards with which I conduct my business.

Ultimately, consistency is key when it comes to incorporating your personal touch. By consistently providing these special elements throughout your interactions with clients, you not only promote your unique qualities, but also build a reputation for exceptional service. Your personal touch becomes synonymous with your brand, leaving a lasting impression on clients and setting the stage for long-term success.

Pre-Booking Appointments

In the fast-paced world of hair and beauty services, client retention is paramount to the success of independent professionals. Securing future appointments before clients leave your salon is a proactive approach to fostering long-term relationships. We will explore the significance of pre-booking and utilising appointment business cards, complete with your logo and contact details. By implementing these practices, you can enhance client satisfaction, reinforce your professional image, and ensure a steady stream of repeat business.

The Value of Pre-Booking

Pre-booking is a proactive strategy that involves scheduling the client's next appointment before they leave your salon. This approach offers numerous benefits. First and foremost, it secures future business, reducing the risk of clients forgetting to book or being swayed by other options. By reserving their spot in advance, you demonstrate your commitment to their ongoing hair and beauty needs, fostering a sense of loyalty and trust.

Enhancing Client Convenience

Pre-booking is a convenient option for clients, saving them time and effort. Rather than having to remember to reach out and schedule their next appointment at a late date, they can leave your salon with peace of mind, knowing their future slot is secured. This streamlined approach shows that you value their time and prioritise their convenience, leaving a positive impression and increasing the likelihood of repeat visits.

Reinforcing Professionalism and Image

Client retention is crucial for sustained success in the hair and beauty industry. By pre-booking appointments and providing appointment business cards, you establish a solid foundation for repeat business. Utilising appointment business cards with your logo and contact details is a powerful tool for reinforcing your professionalism and brand image.

Remember, by securing future appointments and providing appointment business cards, you not only enhance client retention but also reinforce your professional image and increase the likelihood of repeat business. Business cards and promotional material will be discussed on page x. So, take this proactive approach, leaving a lasting impression with every client and establishing yourself as a trusted and reliable provider in the competitive hair and beauty industry.

Appointment Reminders

Imagine you've meticulously planned your day, blocked out the perfect time slot for your client, and prepped your tools like a master chef preps their ingredients. But when the appointed time rolls around, your client is nowhere to be found. Ugh, the dreaded no-show!

Let's dive into why sending reminders is an absolute game-changer.

Reduced No-Shows

Life can get crazy, and appointments can easily slip through the cracks of our clients' busy minds. But fear not, for the text or email reminder is here to save the day! By sending a friendly reminder a few days prior to their appointment, you give clients a gentle nudge to remember and prioritise their commitment. It's like a kind reminder from their fairy godmother (that's you!) to keep their beauty date intact.

Improved Planning and Preparation

With the power of reminders, you can be the ultimate master planner. By knowing in advance which clients will grace your chair, you can allocate the perfect amount of time and resources for each service. No more scrambling or unexpected surprises. It's all about smooth sailing and a well-organised schedule. Your clients will appreciate the extra care and attention you bring to their beauty experience.

Enhanced Communication

Reminders aren't just a one-way street. They provide a golden opportunity for clients to reach out with questions, concerns, or special requests. It's like opening the door to a personalised conversation. By fostering this open line of communication, you can address any queries and make necessary adjustments ahead of time. It's like being a mind reader, but with better hair skills!

Flexibility for Rescheduling

Life can sometimes be a rollercoaster ride, plans change and appointments need to be rescheduled. But with reminders, you give your clients the power of flexibility. They can assess their availability and request a reschedule with ease. By being proactive and accommodating, you're the superhero of their hair dreams.

Demonstration of Professionalism

Sending reminders isn't just about convenience; it's a display of your professionalism. You're showing that you've got your act together, that you're organised like Marie Kondo, and that you respect your clients' time. It's all part of the grand show of delivering top-notch service. When clients see your attention to detail, they'll know they're in the hands of a true pro.

So, let's embrace the power of appointment reminders. They reduce no-shows, improve planning and preparation, enhance client-professional communication, offer convenience and preparation for clients, provide flexibility for rescheduling, and display our undeniable professionalism. It's a win-win situation for everyone involved.

You will find that most online appointment software comes to the rescue with automated reminders and notifications. My preferred online appointment system is Salon Applications Manager (SAM) because sending reminders and keeping in touch with my clients is made super easy with SAM. You can find the contact details to SAM at the end of this guide in the Chapter: My Little Black Book of Contacts. Ask for Andrew and tell him I sent you. He will make sure you are well taken care of.

CELEBRITY HAIRSTYLIST

During the many years of my journey behind the salon chair, I've become a silent witness to countless stories that weave together the lives of those who have graced my salon. Though it's impossible to recall every face and tale, the impact lingers in the hearts and minds of those I've served. Amidst the blur of encounters, some stories stand out vividly. One such tale is of a woman who endured unimaginable loss from a young age, yet emerged as a beacon of resilience. After losing her parents and brother, she found solace amidst grief, channelling her pain into power and refusing to be defined by her circumstances. Today, she inspires as a sought-after professor, her journey from tragedy to triumph is a testament to the human spirit. In the sanctuary of my salon, she shares the raw anguish of her past, a poignant reminder of the light that can emerge from darkness. Through her story, she honours not only her own journey but the resilience within us all. Behind the chair, I strive to be a steadfast support, offering a listening ear and caring presence to each client who I consider stars in their own right on their unique journey of beauty and resilience.

PART FOUR

Building
On Your
Foundation

Balancing the Books

Let's talk about the not-so-glamorous side of our creative ventures: the finances. I know, I know, crunching numbers may not be as exciting as experimenting with new hair colours or giving fabulous makeovers, but trust me, it's just as important. In this section, we're going to dive into the world of financial literacy for freelancers. Don't worry, we'll sprinkle in some personality and a dash of humour to keep things lively.

Mastering Break-Even Analysis

Break-even analysis holds significance for independent freelancers. It serves as a financial compass, guiding you towards informed decision-making regarding pricing strategies, cost management, and overall business sustainability. By calculating the break-even point—which is the level of sales at which total revenues equal total costs—freelancers can determine the minimum sales required to cover their expenses, ensuring you neither incur losses nor leave money on the table. This invaluable tool helps freelancers set competitive prices and understand the financial dynamics of their solo expedition, ultimately contributing to the long-term success and profitability of their business.

Peeking Behind the Scenes With Profit and Loss Statements – Show Me the Money!

The importance of reading a profit and loss statement (P&L) cannot be overstated for freelancers. This document provides an overview of your revenue, expenses and, ultimately, the profitability of your business over a specific period. Freelancers often operate on tight budgets and limited resources; understanding the P&L statement is essential for informed decision-making. It allows you to assess the financial health of your business, pinpoint areas where costs can be controlled or reduced, and gauge the effectiveness of your revenue-generating strategies. It's a vital tool in the toolkit of effective financial management and strategic planning.

Keeping the Taxman Happy

Taxes, my friends, are the necessary evil of doing business. We can navigate this treacherous terrain with confidence. It's all about understanding our tax obligations, getting that fancy Australian Business Number (ABN), and dancing with Business Activity Statements (BAS). And if the GST comes knocking, we'll be ready to show them who's boss.

Staying on top of your tax game keeps the financial ship sailing smoothly, avoids those pesky penalties, and earns you a gold star for professionalism.

The Accountant – Your Financial Fairy Godmother or Godfather

Now, let's talk about our secret weapon in the battle against financial stress: the trusted accountant. These wizards of numbers have the power to unravel complex tax laws, analyse our finances like pros, and offer strategic advice to keep our cash flowing. With their guidance, we can maximise deductions, minimise tax liabilities, and sleep soundly knowing our financial matters are in capable hands.

Accounting Software – The Tech Sidekick

In a world where creativity meets cash flow, financial literacy is our secret weapon. Understanding break-even analysis, mastering profit and loss statements, taming tax obligations, and embracing accounting software empowers us to maintain financial stability and make smart business moves. With the right financial knowledge, trusted accountants, and nifty software by our side, we can focus on what we do best – creating stunning looks and making our clients feel like a million bucks.

There is a number of accounting software that can make running your little business smoother, like Xero and QuickBooks. I have personally found my true companion in Xero. Let me tell you, it's like having a magic wand that banishes all my tax-time anxieties. You can check out plans and pricing for Xero at **www.xero.com.au**.

With my accountant having access to my Xero profile, he simply waltzes in and handles my BAS like it's a piece of cake. And when the glorious end of the financial year arrives, my tax return becomes a breeze for my accountant.

The best part? This software is hooked up to my bank account and trusty EFTPOS machine, creating a seamless journey all the way to my accountant's desk. It's a symphony of streamlined accounting goodness! Say goodbye to headaches and hello to simplified financial harmony.

Salon-Use Products

As a hair and beauty professional, the careful selection of salon-use products plays a vital role in providing exceptional services and ensuring client satisfaction. Balancing quality and cost while offering a memorable experience is a delicate art. Additionally, the potential to retail home-care products opens up exciting avenues for business growth and personal branding.

Let's explore the importance of selecting high-quality salon-use products, and the benefits of retailing home-care products.

Quality and Cost – Striking the Perfect Balance

When it comes to salon-use products, quality should always be a top priority. Opting for reputable brands and professional-grade products ensures you're delivering excellent results to your clients. However, it's equally important to consider the cost implications for your business. Look for product lines that offer a balance between quality and affordability, allowing you to maintain profitability while providing top-notch services. Conduct thorough research, read product reviews, and seek recommendations from trusted industry professionals to make informed decisions.

Retailing Home-Care Products

Retailing home-care products to your clients offers a win-win situation. By recommending products tailored to their specific needs, you provide ongoing care and maintenance beyond their salon visits. This not only helps clients achieve long-lasting results but also generates additional revenue for your business. Select home-care products that align with your salon's services and cater to your clients' preferences.

Building Trust and Loyalty

By using high-quality salon-use products and offering retail home-care products, you build trust and loyalty with your clients. Consistently delivering exceptional results using reliable products creates a positive reputation for your business. As clients experience the benefits of the home-care products you recommend, they develop trust in your expertise and are more likely to rely on your recommendations in the future. The combination of quality salon-use products and retail offerings, establishes you as a trusted authority in the industry.

Effective Marketing and Promotion

To maximise the potential of retailing home-care products and branding your personal line, utilise various channels such as social media, your website, email marketing, and samples to create awareness and generate interest. Highlight the unique benefits of your products, share client success stories, and offer exclusive bundles to incentivise purchases. Engage with your customers, answer their questions, and provide valuable content that promotes the value of your products and services.

Carefully selecting salon-use products that balance quality and cost is essential for delivering exceptional services. Retailing home-care products allows you to extend client care beyond your personal service, generating additional revenue and enhancing client loyalty.

Branded Product Line

Consider and explore opportunities to develop your own line of products as this adds a unique touch to your brand and enhances client loyalty.

Branding Your Retail Products

Taking your freelance business to the next level involves branding your own line of products. This allows you to establish a distinct identity and differentiate yourself from competitors. Consider creating custom formulations, packaging, and labelling that reflect your brand's personality and values. Your personalised products become an extension of your brand and a testament to your expertise and dedication to client care.

Uniqueness and Differentiation

Developing your own branded line of products allows you to offer something truly unique. You can formulate products tailored to your target audience's specific needs, whether it's shampoos for sensitive scalps or conditioners for curly hair. This differentiation sets you apart in a crowded market.

Enhanced Customer Engagement

Customers love to be part of a brand's journey. Involving your customers in the product development process—from choosing scents to testing formulations—can create a sense of ownership and community around your brand.

With years of experience in product research and development, as well as extensive contacts in the manufacturing industry, I am confident in my ability to help you identify the right products for your clients and salon use while also assisting you in creating a unique retail product line that sets you apart from your competitors.

I have a keen eye for identifying opportunities for branding and customisation. With my assistance, we can develop a unique retail product line that bears your salon's name and logo, creating a strong brand identity that resonates with your clients. From custom formulations to captivating packaging design, we can work together to create a line of products that not only enhances client loyalty but also sets you apart from the competition.

Here's how we can work together:

Initial Consultation

We will discuss your specific needs, target market, and brand identity. This will help me gain a deeper understanding of your vision and goals.

Product Research and Selection

I will utilise my expertise and industry contacts to identify the right retail and salon-use products that meet your criteria for quality, cost, and client satisfaction.

Branding and Customisation

We will explore various branding options from personalised packaging to unique formulations, ensuring your retail product line aligns seamlessly with your brand identity.

Manufacturing and Production

Leveraging my contacts in the manufacturing industry, I will oversee the production process to ensure timely delivery and adherence to the highest quality standards.

Marketing and Promotion

Once the retail product line is primed for action, we'll join forces to unleash some marketing magic that will make your products shine brighter than a disco ball. From captivating social media posts to making your goodies available for online retail therapy, and even offering personal promotions with your cherished customers, together we'll create a marketing plan so simple and effective, it'll practically do the cha-cha-cha on its own! Get ready to make your business dreams a reality!

I am genuinely excited about the opportunity to work with you and contribute to the success of your freelance business. My passion for product research and development, coupled with my commitment to excellence, will undoubtedly add value to your business. Reach out now with an email to **ebru@sakssalons.com.au** and we can take it from there.

Creating your own branded haircare range is a strategic move for freelancers in the hair and beauty industry. It not only sets you apart but also allows you to control your brand's narrative, product quality, and profitability. With dedication and a customer-centric approach, your range can become the crown jewel of your freelance business, attracting loyal customers and contributing to your long-term success.

WHISKEY THE CAT

Di's sorrow over the loss of her beloved cat, Whiskey, deeply resonates with me, our shared love for animals binding us together. As scissors snip and colours blend, we mourn together, forging bonds that transcend mere hairstyling. Through this nurturing approach, we become trusted allies in our clients' journey towards self-acceptance and self-love. In moments of vulnerability and connection, true magic happens – tears turn to laughter, and insecurities fade into newfound confidence. Embracing our clients' emotions ensures not only satisfaction but also builds enduring relationships based on trust and compassion. Trust, nurtured with care, is the cornerstone of our profession, leading to fulfillment beyond measure.

Mastering the Art of Cost Reduction and Revenue Growth

In the world of freelancing, where financial freedom and success go hand in hand, mastering the art of cost reduction and revenue growth becomes paramount. As a freelancer, creative thinking plays a pivotal role in maximising profitability and creating a designer life. Let's explore the power of creative thinking and how it can help you cut costs without compromising quality, save time, and uncover opportunities for revenue growth. Join me as we delve into the strategies and tactics that can propel your freelance business to new heights.

Embracing Creative Thinking for Cost Reduction

As a freelancer, it's essential to embrace creativity and cost-effectiveness in every aspect of your business operations. One valuable opportunity lies in making the most of moments of quiet during client interactions. Whether you're blow-drying hair, applying colour, or delivering a facial service, these moments can serve as valuable brainstorming sessions for finding innovative ways to reduce costs while maintaining quality.

This could involve researching and exploring alternative suppliers for salon stock, such as hair dyes, styling products, or skincare ingredients, to find more affordable options without compromising on quality. Additionally, you can assess your current operational processes and identify areas where efficiencies can be improved to reduce overhead costs.

By capitalising on these moments of silence, you can uncover creative solutions to decrease costs and enhance profitability in your freelance business. Embracing a mindset of continuous improvement and resourcefulness not only benefits your bottom line but also reinforces your commitment to delivering high-quality services to your clients. Ultimately, by finding innovative ways to cut costs while maintaining quality, you position yourself for long-term success and sustainability in the competitive hair and beauty industry as a freelancer.

Cutting Costs With DIY Foils, Wax Strips and Smart Purchasing

One practical way to reduce costs is by cutting your own foils if you're a hairdresser instead of purchasing pre-cut ones, and cutting your own wax strips if you offer waxing services as a beautician. By investing a little time in preparing foils and wax strips to your desired size, you can save money while maintaining control over your preferred technique. Additionally, when purchasing salon-use products, tools and equipment from local suppliers, take advantage of your day off to personally order and pick them up. This not only saves on freight costs but also allows you to establish relationships with suppliers, potentially unlocking additional discounts or special offers.

Savvy Shopping for Business Cards and Printed Material

When it comes to business cards and printed material, don't overlook the potential for cost savings. Take the time to shop around, compare prices, and keep an eye out for discounts or vouchers that can be beneficial. Many printing companies offer promotions or bulk pricing, so be sure to explore all available options to secure the best deals while maintaining a professional and polished image for your business.

I have a preferred printing destination called Half Price Printing and I constantly keep an eye out for their periodic promotions that provide printing services at half the regular price. You can find the contact details to Half Price Printing at the back end of this guide in My Little Gold Book of Contacts. Ask for Mem and mention my name. You will be looked after.

Another affordable printing option to consider is Vista. They offer reasonably priced services, and what's even better is that you can design your business cards directly on their website. With a wide range of templates available, the entire process is conveniently handled online.

Revenue Growth Opportunities

Retailing Products

Within the realm of haircare, my haircare brand—Saks Hair—stands as a testament to excellence. Our range transcends the boundaries of the salon, extending its efficacy to the comfort of our clients' homes. Proudly, I am deeply involved in every stage of its creation, collaborating closely with our manufacturers to uphold the uncompromising quality of our ingredients. This dedication ensures that each product within our line is nothing short of exceptional.

At Saks Hair, we firmly believe that beauty should never come at the expense of health. That's why our range is meticulously crafted to be free from any harmful additives, prioritising only the finest ingredients that promote the well-being of both hair and scalp. We address the diverse concerns of our customers with properties carefully selected to nurture and revitalise, leaving them with hair that radiates vitality and health.

However, our commitment doesn't end with the formulation process. We understand the invaluable insight that comes from our customers' experiences, which is why we continually seek their feedback. Their satisfaction is the cornerstone of our ethos, and it fuels our relentless pursuit of excellence. For me, personally, the trust my clients place in the Saks Hair brand is inviolable. It's a reputation built on integrity, and I refuse to compromise it by endorsing anything less than the best.

Retailing products not only generates additional revenue through sales but also contributes to building stronger client relationships and loyalty. When clients trust your expertise and rely on your recommendations for their home-care routines, they're more likely to return to your salon for future services. By offering high-quality products that align with your salon's brand and ethos, you reinforce your commitment to providing comprehensive care and exceptional results to your clients.

Furthermore, retailing products can also serve as a marketing tool for your business. Clients who are satisfied with their results and the products they've purchased are likely to recommend them to friends and family, effectively promoting your salon's brand through word-of-mouth referrals. It's a win-win strategy that not only increases revenue but also strengthens client loyalty, enhances their overall experience, and serves as a marketing tool for your business.

Upselling and Add-On Services

Leverage every client interaction as an opportunity to upsell and offer add-on services. For example, if a client comes in for a haircut, suggest a deep conditioning treatment or scalp massage for an additional fee.

When I recognise that a client's hair is in need of some tender loving care, I take the initiative to offer a complimentary treatment to revive and nourish their locks. By having them feel the power of the treatment, I also recommend they continue the care at home by purchasing a personalised home-care treatment plan. It's a wonderful strategy of giving a little something to create an emotional connection with the recommended products, allowing customers to truly experience and fall in love with them. By incorporating upselling techniques, you can boost your average transaction value and increase your overall revenue.

Remember, success lies in finding unique ways to stand out, delivering exceptional experiences, and continually adapting to meet the evolving needs of your clients.

With dedication, innovation, and a focus on client satisfaction, you can flourish as an independent freelancer while renting space in salons. Get ready to elevate your earnings and take your business to new heights of success!

Next Level Revenue Growth Opportunities

As a freelancer, you have ample opportunities to connect your services with other offerings in the beauty industry. For instance, if you're a hairdresser renting a chair in a salon for three days a week, you might consider adding a day to provide other beauty services in which you're skilled. Alternatively, you could expand your skillset by training in services like eyebrow shaping, lash extensions, or massages.

Especially if your hair business is still in its early stages, combining beauty services on a different day of the week could work well. You might specialise in things like eyelash extensions or facials, and you could even rent a private room within a hair and beauty salon for these services. This integration into the beauty sector could boost your offerings.

Thinking holistically about your clients, you can upsell your beauty services while working on their hair. This multitasking can keep you busy and help you manage all your financial responsibilities, including holidays and savings.

Planning ahead is key, so you can enjoy a well-earned, four-week vacation at the end of the year. Just ensure you're financially prepared to cover that time off.

By staying busy, making the most of your working hours, and finding opportunities to offer additional services and products, you're charting a path toward success in this dynamic fashion-driven industry.

Just The Beginning

As this compendium of years' worth of hard-earned wisdom draws to a close, let me extend my heartfelt congratulations to you for taking the brave leap towards following your dreams, embarking on a solo adventure, and sticking with this guide till the very end. And hey, I'm assuming you didn't cheat and skip straight to this part! (No peeking allowed, haha!)

Now, let's be real – it's not going to be a walk in the park. But guess what? You've chosen a path where you'll be the master of your own destiny, the captain of your own ship. So, when the going gets tough (because it inevitably will), remember to stay resilient and not throw in the towel. Believe me when I say, "If I can do it, anyone can!"

And hey, here's a little secret: If at any point along your journey, you find yourself yearning for a listening ear, an extra pair of hands, or a fresh perspective, don't hesitate to reach out. I'd be absolutely delighted to lend my support as someone who's walked this path before you. Consider me your trusty sounding board, always ready to assist you along the way. You never have to feel alone on this adventure.

So, with a heart full of excitement and anticipation, let's embrace this journey together, knowing that you've armed yourself with valuable knowledge.

Here's to chasing your dreams and carving out your own path – it's going to be one epic ride!

With Love,

Ebru Sak

LOVE FROM WITHIN

Love is a powerful emotion that can inspire us to be kind, compassionate, and understanding towards others and to ourselves. When we approach life with love, we are more likely to see the beauty and goodness in the world around us. We are more likely to be optimistic, grateful, and content with what we have rather than constantly striving for more.

When we approach challenges with love, we are more likely to be patient, understanding, and forgiving towards ourselves and others. This can help us to stay calm and focused even in the face of adversity.

Food for thought.

MY LITTLE GOLD BOOK OF CONTACTS

Register your Business Name
www.connectonline.asic.gov.au

Australian Business Register – ABR
www.abr.business.gov.au

Australian Taxation Office – ATO
www.ato.gov.au

Trademark and Intellectual Property
www.ipaustralia.gov.au

WKK Insurance Advisors
www.wkkinsurance.com.au

Appointment Booking Software
www.australiapos.com.au

Accountant & Tax Agent
John Paterno CPA
0459 129 829

Xero Accounting Software
www.xero.com.au

Website Creating Platform
www.wix.com

Half Price Printing
www.halfpriceprinting.com.au

Vista Printing
www.vistaprint.com.au

CONTACT AUTHOR

My salon business is **www.sakssalons.com.au**

My makeup brand is **www.marquage.com.au**

My personal website is **www.ebrusak.com**

www.ingramcontent.com/pod-product-compliance
Lightning Source LLC
Chambersburg PA
CBHW041300040426
42334CB00028BA/3094